Jungle Tales

Jungle Tales

Written by Horacio Quiroga

Published by Creolio

   10347 Butternut Circle Manassas, VA 20110

   creolio.com

Translator

   Jon Knebel (U. S. A.)

Book Cover

   Juan Pablo Zorrilla (Uruguay)

Chapter Illustrations

   Lucas Roselli (Uruguay)

Table of Contents

About the Author & Stories

The eight stories were written by Horacio Quiroga in 1918 — a famous Uruguayan author and known influence upon the "magical realism" of such authors as Gabriel García Márquez, who wrote "100 Years of Solitude" and "Love in the Time of Cholera".

The stories are suitable for children through adults because, while they feature talking animals in the fun contexts of the jungle and use language, the stories go deeper than they first appear and can appeal to the mature reader as well.

Modernized & Standardized

"Jungle Tales" is a simplified and fairly word-for-word translation of "Cuentos de la Selva" (1918) by Horacio Quiroga of Uruguay.

Before being translated into English, the stories were simplified in the original Spanish, modernized, standardized, and colloquialisms were removed. This was to create a version of the book that would be easiest to read for the broadest audience of readers, including younger children. When translating into English, the story was kept word-for-word as often as possible to preserve the Spanish style and to help prepare the English reader for the Spanish way of thinking.

The Stories

The Story of Two Coati Pups and Two Man Pups

There was once a coati that had three children. They lived in the jungle and would eat fruits, roots and birds' eggs. When they were up in the trees and would hear a loud noise, they would throw themselves to the ground headlong and run away with their tails raised.

When the little coatis got a little bigger, their mother got them together one day up in an orange tree and spoke to them:

"Little coatis, you are big enough to look for food by yourselves. You should learn to do it because when you're old you'll go about by yourselves like all coatis. The first of you, whom it pleases to hunt insects, can find them among the rotten sticks, since there are many beetles and cockroaches there. The second one, who is a great eater of fruits, can find them in this orange grove since oranges grow here until December. The third one, who doesn't like to eat anything except birds' eggs, can go everywhere — since everywhere there are birds' nests — but might he never go into the field to look for nests — it's dangerous.

"Little coatis: there's one single thing of which you should have great fear: dogs. I fought once with them and I know what I'm saying to you: because of that fight I have a broken tooth. Behind the dogs always come the men with a great noise that kills. When you hear this noise nearby, throw yourselves headlong to the ground, even if the tree which you are in is very tall. If you don't do this, they'll certainly kill you with one shot."

So spoke the mother. Everyone got down then and parted ways, walking from right to left and from left to right as if they'd lost something — because coatis walk in this way.

The first one, who liked to eat insects, searched among the rotten sticks and the leaves of the herbs and found so many beetles and cockroaches that he ate until falling asleep. The second one, who liked fruit more than anything, ate all the oranges that he could want because the orange grove was inside of the jungle as is the case in Paraguay and in Misiones, and no man came to cause him problems. The third one, who was crazy for birds' eggs, had to go about all day in order to find just two nests: one of a toucan which had three eggs and one of a heron which had only two. In total, five very small eggs was very little food. At evening, the little coati was as hungry as he was in the morning, and he sat at the edge of the jungle, very sad. From that vantage point, he saw the field and thought on his mother's warning.

"Why doesn't mama want," he told himself, "for me to go look for nests in the field?"

He was thinking in this way when he heard — very far off — the crow of a bird.

"What a loud crow!" he said excitedly. "What giant eggs that bird must have!"

The crow repeated itself. Then, the coati ran through the jungle and took a shortcut because the crow had come from his right. The sun was setting already, but the coati was nearly flying with his tail raised. He arrived at the edge of the jungle at last, and he looked to the field: far off, he saw a house and he saw a man wearing boots that was riding a burro. He also saw a very big bird that was crowing. Then the little coati hit himself on the head and said:

"How silly I am! I already know what bird it is. It's a rooster. Mama showed me one once from up in a tree. Roosters have a very nice crow and have many chickens that lay eggs. If only I could eat chicken eggs!"

It's well known that nothing pleases the small creatures of the jungle so much as chicken eggs. After a while, the little coati reminded himself of his mother's warning, but his desire was stronger, and he sat at the edge of the jungle and waited until nightfall in order to go to the chicken coop.

Night arrived at last. Then slowly, and step by step, he walked toward the house. He arrived there and listened attentively: he didn't hear the least sound. The little coati was crazy with joy because he was going to eat one hundred, one thousand, even six thousand chicken eggs. He entered into the chicken coop and the first thing that he saw in the entrance was an egg that was alone on the ground. He thought for an instant on leaving it for dessert because it was a very large egg, but it made his mouth water, so he bit into the egg with his teeth.

As soon as he bit it, there was a "Whack!" He received a terrible hit on his head and felt an immense pain in his face.

"Mama, mama!" he shouted, crazy from pain and jumping all over the place. He was held in place and — at that moment — he heard the rough bark of a dog.

While the coati had been waiting for night at the edge of the jungle in order to go to the chicken coop, the man of the house had been playing upon the grass with his children: two kids of five and six years who were running, laughing, falling down, getting up, laughing once again, and returning to fall down again. The father was falling down too — giving great joy to the kids. Finally, they stopped playing because it was already nighttime and the man said:

"I'm going to place the trap in order to catch the mongoose that has been coming to kill the little chickens and rob their eggs."

He went and placed the trap. Afterward, they ate and put themselves to bed, but the kids couldn't sleep: they were jumping from one bed to another and were entangling themselves in their pajamas. The father, who was reading in the dining room, let them do it; nevertheless, the kids suddenly stopped in their jumps and shouted:

"Papa! The mongoose has fallen in the trap! The dog is barking! We want to go see also, papa!"

The father consented, but not without having the kids put on their boots because he would never let them go about without boots at night for fear of the vipers.

They went. What did they see there? They saw their father who was crouching and holding the dog with one hand, while with the other he was lifting a coati by the tail — a small coati indeed, who was making a loud and strident squeal.

"Papa, don't kill it!" said the kids. "It's little! Give it to us!"

"Well, I'll give it to you," responded the father. "Care for it well, and — above all — don't forget that coatis drink water like you."

The father said this to them because the kids had once had a little wildcat to which they continually gave meat, but they never gave it water, and it died of thirst.

In consequence, they put the coati in the same cage as the wildcat, which was close to the chicken coop, and everyone went to bed once again.

When it was past midnight and there was a great silence, the little coati, who was suffering greatly because of the teeth of the trap, saw, by the light of the moon, three dark silhouettes that were approaching carefully. The poor little coati was thrilled upon recognizing his mother and his two brothers that were looking for him.

"Mama, mama!" murmured the prisoner in a very quiet voice in order not to make noise. "I'm here! Get me out of here! I don't want to stay, mama!" He was crying inconsolably, but in spite of everything they were glad because they had found each other, and they gave each other a thousand caresses on the face.

Straightaway, they tried to free the prisoner. First, they tried to cut the wire. The four of them began to work at it with their teeth, but they weren't achieving anything. Suddenly, an idea occurred to the mother and she said:

"Let's look for the man's file! Men have things for cutting metal. They're called files. They have three sides like a rattlesnake. You push it backward and forward in order to cut. Let's go find it!"

They went to the man's stables and returned with the file. Knowing that one alone wouldn't have enough strength to do it, they held the file among the three of them and started to work. They got so excited that—after a while—the entire cage was trembling, and it was making a terrible noise. It was making so much noise that the dog woke up and launched a rough bark, so the coatis didn't wait around for the dog to pursue them and ran to the jungle, leaving the file thrown aside.

The following day, the kids went early in the morning to see their new guest, who was very sad.

"What name will we give it?" asked the girl to her brother.

"I know!" responded the boy. "We'll name him Seventeen!"

Why Seventeen? Never was there a jungle creature with a stranger name, but the little boy was learning to count, and it's possible that that number had called to his attention.

So his name was Seventeen. They gave him bread, fruit (including bananas and oranges), chocolate, meat, insects (including beetles and cockroaches), and the most tasty chicken eggs. So great was the sincerity of the kids' affection that, when night came, the coati had almost accepted his captivity. He liked to think about the tasty things that there were to eat there and about these man-pups who were so joyful and good.

During two subsequent nights, the dog slept so close to the cage that the family of the prisoner couldn't try to approach — to their great sorrow. When they arrived again on the third night to look for the file so that they might free the little coati, he told them:

"Mama: I don't want to go from here anymore. They give me eggs and are very good to me. Today they told me that if I would behave myself well they were going to let me loose very soon. They're like us. They're pups too and we play together."

Upon hearing this, the wild coatis became very sad, but they resigned themselves to it and promised to the little coati to come every night to visit him.

Effectively, every night, whether it would rain or not, his mother and his brothers would come to spend a while with him. The little coati would give them bread through the wire and the wild coatis would sit to eat in front of the cage.

After fifteen days had passed, the little coati was allowed to go about free during the day, but would come back at night to his cage. At times, the chickens would peck his ears when he would walk close to the chicken coop, but—besides this— everything was going well. He and the kids loved each other very much, and the wild coatis, upon seeing how good that those man-pups were, ended up by having affection for the two children also.

One very dark and rainy night when it was very hot, the wild coatis called to the little coati and nobody answered them. Then they approached the cage very restlessly and saw, when almost stepping on it, an enormous viper that was curled up at the entrance of the cage. The coatis understood straightaway that the little coati had been bitten upon entering and had not answered their call because he was possibly already dead. They were going to avenge him well. In a second, among the three of them, they made the rattlesnake get angry by jumping from here to there, and, in another second, they fell upon it, tearing its head apart with bites.

Then they ran inside, and indeed the little coati was lying there, swollen, with his paws trembling, and he was dying. In vain the wild coatis tried to move him; they licked him all over his body for a quarter of an hour. Then the little coati finally opened his mouth and stopped breathing because he was dead.

Coatis are almost immune, as is said, to the venom of vipers, and venom does almost nothing to them. There are also other animals like this — like the mongoose — that resist the venom of vipers very well. With complete certainty, the little coati had been bitten in an artery or a vein. In such cases, the blood gets poisoned straightaway and the animal dies. This had happened to the little coati.

Upon seeing him like this, his mother and brothers cried a long while. Afterward, as there was nothing more they could do there, they went out of the cage, turned around in order to look at the house for the last time where the little coati had been so happy, and they went from there once again to the jungle. The three coatis went along very restlessly. What were the kids going to say when, the following day, they would see their beloved little coati dead? The kids loved him greatly and they, the coatis, also loved the man-pups. So it is that the three coatis had the same thought, and it was to prevent that great heartache to those kids.

They talked a long while and finally decided upon the following: the second of the coatis, who greatly resembled the youngest in body and manner of being, went to stay in the cage in place of the dead one. As they knew many secrets of the house because of what the little coati had told them, the kids wouldn't know the difference; they would notice some small things that were different, but nothing else.

So it happened indeed. They returned to the house and a new little coati substituted the first one while the mother and the other brother were going from there with the body of the youngest coati held between their teeth. They slowly took him to the jungle while his head was hanging down and his tail was dragging over the ground.

The following day, the kids noticed — effectively — some strange habits of the little coati, but as this one was just as good and caring as the other, the kids didn't end up having the least suspicion. They formed the same family of pups as before and — as before — the wild coatis would come night after night to visit the domesticated coati and would sit at his side to eat little pieces of eggs that he would save for them while they would tell him about their lives in the jungle.

The End

The Blind Fawn

There was once a doe that had two identical daughters, which is a rare thing among deer. A wildcat ate one of the female fawns and only the other female fawn remained. The other does, who loved her greatly, would always nuzzle her on her sides. Her mother would make her repeat the saying of the deer very early every morning. It goes like this:

I

One has to smell the leaves thoroughly first before eating them because some are poisonous.

II

One has to observe the river thoroughly and stay still before going down to drink in order to be sure that there are no alligators.

III

Every half hour, one has to lift one's head very high and smell the wind in order to smell if there's the smell of jaguar.

IV

When grass is eaten from the ground, one has to always look at the bushes in order to see if there are vipers.

This is the saying of the small deer. When the fawn learned it well, her mother let her go about by herself.

One afternoon, while the fawn was roaming the jungle and eating the tender little leaves, suddenly she saw before her, in the hollow of a tree that was rotten, many little balls that were hanging together. They had a dark color like that of obsidian.

What could it be? She also was a little afraid, but as she was very curious, she gave a hit with her head at those things.

She saw then that the little balls had opened up and that drops of something were falling. There had come out also many insects with very thin waists that were walking quickly.

The fawn approached and the little flies didn't sting her. Then, slowly, very slowly, she touched a drop with the tip of her tongue and salivated with great desire: those drops were honey — honey super tasty — the black balls were little bees that don't sting, since they didn't have stingers. There are bees like that.

In two minutes, the fawn drank all the honey and, crazy from happiness, went to tell her mama; nevertheless, her mama seriously warned her.

"Take great care, my daughter," she said to her, "with beehives. Honey is a very tasty thing, but it's very dangerous to remove it. Never stick your nose into the beehives that you see."

The fawn shouted happily:

"They don't sting, mama! Other insects do sting, but bees don't sting."

"That's not the truth, my daughter," continued the mother. "Yes there are bees that don't sting, but there are very bad bees and wasps too. Take care, my daughter, because you're going to give me a great displeasure."

"Yes, mama! Yes, mama!" responded the fawn, but the first thing that she did the following morning was to follow the paths that the men had opened in the jungle in order to see the beehives more easily.

She finally found one. This time, the hive had dark bees with a yellow belt on their waists that were walking over top of the beehive. The hive was also different; however, the fawn thought that due to the fact that these bees were bigger, the honey should be tastier.

Furthermore, she reminded herself of the warning of her mama, but thought that she was exaggerating like the mothers of the other fawns who always exaggerate. Then, she gave a great headbutt to the beehive.

If only she had never done it! Hundreds of wasps came out straightaway—thousands of wasps stung her all over her body. They stung her on the head, on the abdomen, on the tail and, what is much worse, on the eyes. More than ten stung her in the eyes.

"Mama! Mama!"

Her mother, who had gone out to look for her because she was taking a long time, finally found her, and despaired also with her fawn who was blind. She took her step by step up to her den with the head of her daughter inclined upon her neck. All the creatures of the jungle that they encountered on the way would approach, wanting to see the eyes of the unhappy fawn.

The mother didn't know what to do. What remedies could she prepare for her? She knew that in the town at the other side of the jungle was living a man who had remedies. The man was a hunter, and sometimes would hunt deer also, but he was a good man.

The mother was afraid to bring her daughter to a man who hunted deer. As she was desperate she made up her mind to do it, but before doing so she wanted to go ask for a letter of recommendation from the anteater, who was a great friend of the man.

She left after leaving the fawn thoroughly hidden and ran through the jungle, where a jaguar almost overtook her on the way. When she arrived at the den of her friend, she couldn't take one more step because she was so exhausted.

This friend was, as has been said, an anteater. It was of a small, yellow species that has a type of black shirt that goes over top of its shoulders. This species also has a flexible tail that allows them to live in the trees and hang from their tails.

Why were the anteater and the hunter friends? Nobody knew in the jungle, but someday we'll know the reason.

The poor mother made it up to the den of the anteater.

"Knock! Knock! Knock!"

"Who is it," responded the anteater.

"It is I, the doe!"

"Ah, well! What does the doe want?" said the anteater.

"I come to ask you for a letter of recommendation for the hunter. The fawn, my daughter, is blind," said the doe.

"Ah, the fawn?" responded the anteater to her. "She's a good person. If it's for her, then yes I'll give you what you want, but you don't need anything written... Just show him this and he'll try to cure her," said the anteater.

And with the tip of his tail, the anteater extended to the doe a dry viper's head — completely dry — that still had its poisonous teeth.

"Show him this," said still the eater of ants. "Nothing more is needed."

"Thank you, anteater!" happily responded the doe. "You also are a good person."

And she left running, since it was very late and soon the sun was going to go down.

Upon passing by her den, she reunited herself with her daughter, who was crying continually, and they arrived together at last to the town. They had to walk very slowly and keep close to the houses so that the dogs wouldn't smell them. They were already before the door of the hunter.

"Knock! Knock! Knock!"

"What's up?" responded the voice of a man from inside.

"We're the does! We have the viper's head!"

The mother rushed to say this so that the man would know that they were friends of the anteater.

"Ah, ah!" said the man as he opened the door. "What's happening?"

"We came so that you might cure my daughter, the fawn, who is blind," said the mother.

And she told the hunter the whole story of the bees.

"Hmm!... Let's see what this little lady has," said the hunter. He went back to enter into the house, came out again with a high chair, and made the fawn sit in it in order to be able to see her eyes better without having to crouch too much. He examined her eyes closely with a very large pair of glasses while the mama gave some light with a lantern she hung from her neck.

"This is not a big deal," said the hunter at last, while helping the fawn to get down. "One has to have much patience. Put this cream in her eyes every night and keep her in the darkness for twenty days. Afterward, put these yellow glasses on her and she'll be cured."

"Many thanks, hunter!" responded the mother very glad and thankful. "How much do I owe you?"

"It's nothing," responded the happy hunter. "Be careful about the dogs because in the other block lives a man that has dogs for following the scent of deer."

The does were very afraid. After almost each step, they would have to stop. In spite of all this effort, the dogs still smelled them and pursued them for three kilometers into the jungle. They were running by a very large path and the fawn went from there complaining.

Like the hunter said, the cure worked, but only the doe knew how much it costed her to have enclosed the fawn in the hollow of a big tree for those twenty endless days. Inside, she couldn't see at all. Finally, one morning, the mother parted with her head the great pile of branches that she had moved closer to the hollow of the tree so that light wouldn't enter, and the fawn, with her yellow glasses, left running and was shouting:

"I see, mama! Already I can see everything!"

And the doe inclined her head on a branch — she was crying from joy at seeing her fawn cured.

And she was healed altogether, but cured and happy, the fawn had a secret that saddened her. And the secret was this: she wanted at all costs to compensate the man who had been so good to her, but she didn't know how.

One day, she believed to have found the means. She roamed the banks of the lagoons and looked for heron feathers in order to bring them to the hunter. The hunter, for his part, thought of that blind fawn that he had cured from time to time.

One rainy night, the man was reading in his room and was very glad because he had just finished repairing the straw roof that now would prevent the rain from entering when he heard that someone was knocking. He opened the door and saw the fawn with some wet heron feathers.

The hunter laughed, and the fawn, humiliated because she believed that the hunter was laughing at her wet feathers, went away from there very sad. She then sought very big feathers that were very dry and intact, and a week later she returned with them. This time the man, who had laughed the last time out of affection, didn't laugh this time because he knew that the fawn didn't understand his laughter. He gave her a tube of bamboo full of honey that the fawn drank crazy from happiness.

Since then, the fawn and the hunter were great friends. She would always insist on bringing him valuable heron feathers, and she would stay for hours chatting with the man. He would always put a jar full of honey upon the table and would move the little high chair close for his friend. At times, he would also give her cigars, which deer eat with great pleasure (and don't make them sick). They would spend the time like this, watching the fire, since the man had a stove while the wind and the rain outside were shaking the straw roof of the hut.

Owing to her fear of the dogs, the fawn would go only on rainy nights. And when evening would come and it would start to rain, the hunter would set on the table the little jar of honey, while he would drink coffee and read, awaiting on the door the well known "knock-knock" of his friend the fawn.

The End

The War of the Alligators

In a very large river, in a deserted region where man had never been, many alligators were living. They were more than a hundred or more than a thousand. They would eat fish and animals that would go to drink water at the river, but above all fish. They would sleep the siesta on the sand of the bank and at times they would play upon the water when the nights were moonlit.

All of them were living very calm and happy, but one afternoon while they were sleeping the siesta, an alligator woke up suddenly and lifted its head because it thought it had heard a noise. It listened and far away — very far away — it heard a low and muffled noise. Then he called to the alligator that was sleeping at his side.

"Wake up!" he said to him. "There's danger."

"What danger?" responded the other, frightened.

"I don't know," answered the alligator that had woken up first. "I hear a noise that I don't recognize."

The second alligator heard the noise at the same time and in a moment they woke the others. Everyone got scared and was running from one side to another with their tails raised.

And they had reason to be restless because the noise was growing and growing. Soon, they saw what seemed like a little cloud of smoke in the distance and heard a noise of "slap-slap" in the river as if something was hitting the water very far away.

The alligators looked at each other: What could that be? An old and wise alligator—the most wise and old of all, an old alligator to whom didn't remain but two teeth on the sides of his mouth and that had once made a trip to the sea—suddenly said:

"I know what it is! It's a whale! They're big and they blow white water up into the air, which then splashes back into the river."

Upon hearing this, the small alligators started to shout like crazy from fear, submerging their heads. They were shouting:

"It's a whale! Here comes the whale!" Then the old alligator shook his tail at the nearest little alligator.

"Don't be afraid!" he shouted to them. "I know what the whale is! She is afraid of us! She's always afraid!"

With this, the small alligators calmed down, but straightaway they went back to being scared because the gray smoke converted suddenly into black smoke and all felt the "slap-slap-slap" very strong now in the water. The alligators, scared, sank themselves into the river and left only their eyes and the point of their noses above the water. And so they saw pass in front of them that immense thing full of smoke that was hitting the water: it was a steam ship which was navigating for the first time by that river.

The ship passed, withdrew and disappeared. Then the alligators were coming out of the water very angry with the old alligator since he had mislead them in telling them that it was a whale.

"That is not a whale! they shouted to him in his ears because he was a bit deaf. "What is that thing that passed?"

The old alligator then explained to them that it was a steam ship, full of fire, and that all the alligators were going to die if the ship would continue passing, but the alligators laughed because they thought that the old gator had gone crazy. Why were they going to die if the ship would continue passing? He was quite crazy, the poor old alligator!

As they were hungry, they began to look for fish, but there wasn't even one — they didn't find a single fish. All had gone away — scared by the noise of the ship. There weren't anymore fish.

"Wasn't I saying this to you?" said the old alligator then. "No longer do we have anything to eat. All the fish have gone from here. Let's wait until tomorrow. It could be that the ship might not come back anymore and the fish might return when they're not afraid anymore."

But the following day, they heard the noise in the water again and saw the ship pass, making lots of noise and throwing so much smoke that it was obscuring the sky.

"Well," said the alligators; "the ship passed before, it passed today and it will pass tomorrow. No longer will there be anymore fish or animals to come drink water, and we'll die of hunger. Let's make a dike then."

"Yes, a dike! A dike!" shouted everyone, swimming at full force toward the bank. "Let's make a dike!"

Straightaway they made the dike. Everyone went to the jungle and they threw down more than ten thousand trees — above all very strong trees... They cut them with the type of saw that alligators have on top of their tails and pushed them to the water, placing them from one side to the other of the river, with a meter of distance between each one. No ship could pass by there, neither big nor small. They were sure that nobody would come to scare the fish. Then, as they were very tired, they laid down to sleep on the beach.

The following day, they were still sleeping when they heard the "slap-slap-slap" of the ship. Everyone heard, but nobody got up or even opened their eyes. How would the ship affect them? It could make all the noise that it wanted, but it wasn't going to pass by there.

Indeed: the ship was very far away still when it stopped. The men that were inside saw that thing in the middle of the river with binoculars and took a boat in order to see what it was that was impeding them from passing. Then the alligators got up, went to the dike, watched from between the sticks, and were laughing at the frustration that the ship had brought upon itself.

The boat approached, saw the formidable dike that the alligators had raised and returned to the ship, but afterward it came back once again to the dike, and the men of the boat shouted:

"Eh, alligators!"

"What's up?!" responded the alligators, and they stuck out their heads from between the trunks of the dike.

"That is impeding us to pass!" continued the men.

"We already know it!" said the alligators.

"We can't pass!"

"That's what we want!"

"Remove the dike!" Shouted the men.

"We won't remove it!"

The men of the boat spoke a while in a quiet voice amongst them and shouted afterward:

"Alligators!"

"What's up?" they answered them.

"You won't remove it?"

"No!"

"Until tomorrow, then!" said the men.

"Until when you want!" taunted the alligators.

And the boat returned to the ship while the alligators — crazy from happiness — made enormous slaps in the water. No ship was going to pass by there, and always — always — there would be fish. But the following day, the ship returned, and when the alligators looked at the ship, they fell into silence from surprise: it wasn't the same ship. It was another, much bigger ship than the other. What new ship was it? That ship also wanted to pass? It wasn't going to pass, no. Neither that one, nor another, nor any other!

"No, it's not going to pass!" shouted the alligators while launching themselves to the dike, each one to its place between the trunks.

The new ship, like the other, stopped far away, and also, like the other, lowered a boat that approached the dike. Inside were coming an official and eight sailors. The official shouted:

"Eh, alligators!"

"What's up?!" they responded.

"You won't remove the dike?" said the official.

"No."

"No?"

"No!" shouted the alligators.

"It's okay," said the official. "Then, we're going to sink it with our cannons."

"Shoot away!" answered the alligators.

And the boat returned to the ship.

Now well, that ship was a warship — a battleship with terrible cannons. The wise old alligator that had gone once to the sea remembered suddenly, and barely had time to shout to the other alligators:

"Hide yourselves under the water! Quickly! It's a warship! Careful! Hide yourselves!"

The alligators disappeared in an instant under the water and swam toward the bank where they kept submerged with only their noses and eyes outside of the water. In that same moment, a great white cloud of smoke came out of the ship. It made a terrible noise, and an enormous cannon shot fell on the dike — right in the middle. Two or three trunks flew into pieces. Straightaway fell another shot and another and another one: each one was making a piece of the dike jump through the air in splinters until nothing remained of the dike. Neither a trunk nor a splinter remained. Everything had been destroyed with by the cannons of the battleship. Then the alligators, submerged in the water, with only their eyes and noses outside of it, saw the warship pass, steaming at full force.

Then the alligators came out of the water and said:

"Let's make another dike — bigger than the other one."

And in that same afternoon and night, they made another dike with immense trunks. Afterward, they laid down to sleep, super tired, and they were still sleeping the following day when the warship arrived once again and the boat approached the dike.

"Eh, alligators!" shouted the official.

"What's up?!" responded the alligators.

"Remove that other dike!" scolded the official.

"We won't remove it!"

"We're going to destroy it with cannon shots like the other one!" he warned.

"Destroy it... if you can!" jeered the alligators.

And they spoke like this with arrogance because they were sure that their new dike could not be destroyed even by all the cannons of the earth, but a while afterward the ship filled itself with smoke again and, with a horrible noise, a shot exploded in the middle of the dike. This time they had used a grenade. The grenade exploded against the trunks, and made them jump. It cut the enormous trunks to splinters. The second grenade exploded next to the first, and another piece of dike flew through the air. So they went destroying the dike until nothing remained of it—nothing. The warship then passed in front of the alligators and the men taunted them.

"Well," said the alligators coming out of the water. "We're going to die because the ship is going to pass by forever and the fish won't return either."

They were sad because the little alligators were hungry. Then, the old alligator said:

"We still have a hope of saving ourselves. Let's go see the Catfish. I made a trip with him when I went up to the sea and he has a torpedo. He saw a fight between two warships and brought a torpedo here that didn't manage to explode. Let's go ask him for it. Although he's very angry with us alligators, he's good and won't want for all of us to die."

The fact is that before—many years before—the alligators had eaten a grandson of the Catfish and he hadn't wanted to have anymore relations with them because of this, but, in spite of everything, they went running to see the Catfish, who was living in a massive cave on the bank of the Parana river, and who would always sleep beside his torpedo.

There are catfish that get up to two meters in length, and the owner of the torpedo was one of those.

"Eh, Catfish!" shouted all the alligators from the entrance of the cave, not trying to enter because of that incident with the grandson.

"Who calls?" answered the Catfish.

"It's us, the alligators!"

"I don't have nor do I want to have relation with you," responded the Catfish in a bad mood.

Then, the old alligator brought himself forward a bit into the cave and said:

"It is I, Catfish! I'm your friend the alligator that made the trip with you up to the sea!"

Upon hearing that familiar voice, the Catfish came out of the cave.

"Ah, I had not recognized you!" he said to him affectionately. "What do you want?"

"We came to ask you for the torpedo. There's a warship that passes by our river and it's scaring the fish. It's a warship—a battleship. We made a dike and it sunk it. We made another and it sunk that also. The fish have left and we're on the way to die of hunger. Please, give us the torpedo, and we'll shoot it."

The Catfish, upon hearing this, thought a long while and afterward said:

"It's okay... I'll give you the torpedo, although I always remind myself of what you did with my grandson. Who knows how to make the torpedo explode?"

Nobody knew and everyone became quiet.

"It's okay," said the Catfish with satisfaction, "I will make it explode. I know how to do this."

Then they organized the trip. The alligators held onto each other — from the tail of one to the neck of the other and from the tail of this one to the neck of that one — forming thus a long column of alligators more than one hundred meters long. The immense Catfish pushed the torpedo toward the current and placed himself beneath it, holding it upon his back so that it would float. When they had finished tying together the alligators one after the other, the Catfish fastened himself by the teeth to the tail of the last alligator, and like so they started the march. The Catfish was holding the torpedo and the alligators were dragging it while they were running along the riverbank. They were going up, they were going down, they were jumping upon the rocks. They were always running and they were dragging the torpedo which was making foam like a ship because of the speed of their running. The following morning, very early, they arrived at the place where they had constructed their last dike. Then they started another dike straightaway, but it was much stronger than the ones before it because they followed the suggestion of the Catfish to place the trunks close together, one at the side of another. It was a truly formidable dike.

It was scarcely an hour since they just finished setting the last trunk of the dike when the warship appeared once again and the boat with the official and eight sailors approached the dike again. The alligators climbed up the trunks and stuck out their heads through the other side.

"Eh, alligators!" shouted the official.

"What's up?!" responded the alligators.

"Once again the dike?"

"Yes, once again!"

"Remove that dike!" said the official.

"Never!"

"You won't remove it?"

"No!" yelled the alligators.

"Well then, listen," said the official. "We're going to destroy this dike, and so that you don't make another, we're going to destroy you afterward as well with our cannons. Not even one single one of you is going to remain alive: neither big nor small, neither young nor old... like that super old alligator that I see there and who doesn't have but two teeth on the sides of his mouth."

The old and wise alligator, upon seeing that the official was talking about him and was mocking, said to him:

"It's true that only a few teeth remain to me — and some are broken. But do you know what these teeth are going to eat tomorrow?" he said opening his immense mouth.

"What are they going to eat, I wonder?" responded the sailors.

"That little official," said the alligator, and he got down quickly from his trunk.

Meanwhile, the Catfish had placed his torpedo in the middle of the dike and ordered four alligators to secure it with care and to sink it in the water until the moment in which he would tell them to release it. So they did. The remaining alligators submerged themselves at the same time close to the bank and left only their noses and eyes outside of the water. The Catfish submerged himself at the side of his torpedo.

Suddenly the warship filled itself up with smoke and launched the first cannon shot against the dike. The grenade exploded right in the center of the dike and made ten or twelve trunks fly into a thousand pieces, but the Catfish was alert and, as soon as the hole was made in the dike, he shouted to the alligators that were under the water holding the torpedo:

"Release the torpedo quickly — release it!"

The alligators released it and the torpedo surfaced.

In less time than is needed in order to tell about it, the Catfish placed the torpedo in the center of the open hole, aimed with one eye, put in motion the mechanism of the torpedo, and launched it against the ship.

It was about time! In that instant the battleship launched its second cannon shot and the grenade was going to explode among the sticks, making another piece of the dike jump into splinters, but the torpedo was arriving to the ship and the men that were in it saw it. That is to say, they saw the foam that a torpedo makes in the water. They all gave a great shout of fear and tried to move the battleship so that the torpedo wouldn't hit it, but it was too late: the torpedo arrived, hit the immense ship in the center, and exploded.

It's not possible to relate the terrible noise with which the torpedo exploded. It exploded and broke the ship into fifteen thousand pieces: it launched cannons, boats, and everything else hundreds and hundreds of meters into the air.

The alligators gave a shout of triumph and ran like crazy to the dike. From there, they saw the dead, injured, and alive men pass through the hole that was opened by the grenade. The current of the river was dragging them.

The alligators climbed onto the two trunks that remained on the two sides of the hole and when the men were passing through there, they would mock them.

They didn't want to eat any of the men, although it might've been justified. Only when one passed by that had cords of gold in his suit and who was alive, the old alligator jumped to the water and "chomp!" In two bites he ate him whole.

"Who is that?" asked an ignorant little alligator.

"It's the official," answered the Catfish to it. "My old friend had promised him that he was going to eat him and he has done it."

The alligators removed the rest of the dike, which no longer was good for anything, since no ship would return to pass by there. The Catfish, who had fallen in love with the belt and the cords of the official, asked them to give them to him, and had to remove them from between the teeth of the old alligator, since they had gotten tangled there. The Catfish put on the belt and the cords and secured them around his body. Since the Catfish' skin is very nice and the dark stripes that it has resemble the stripes of a viper, the Catfish swam for an hour passing back and forth before the alligators, who were admiring him with their mouths open.

Then the alligators accompanied him to his cave and gave him a thousand thanks. They returned afterward to their own place. The fish returned too, and the alligators lived and still live very happy because in the end they've accustomed themselves to see ships pass by that bring oranges, but they don't want to know anything about ships of war.

The End

The Plucked Parrot

There was once a group of parrots that lived in the jungle.

Early in the morning, they would go eat corn at the ranch and in the afternoon, they would eat oranges. They would make lots of noise with their squawks and would always have a guard parrot in the tallest trees that to see when humans were coming.

Parrots are as destructive as insects because they open the corn in order to peck at it which, afterward, rots in the rain. Because of this, and since parrots are good to eat, the workers would hunt them with shotguns.

One day, a man brought down a guard parrot with one shot, which fell wounded and fought a good while before letting itself be grabbed. The worker brought him to the house in order to bring him to the children of the landlord, who cured him because he didn't have more than a broken wing. The parrot got better and was completely domesticated. They called him Pedrito. He learned to greet with his leg, and he liked to be on people's shoulders and to peck at their ears.

He lived freely and would spend almost all day among the orange and eucalyptus trees of the garden. He also liked to tease the chickens. At the fourth or fifth hour of the afternoon, which was the time when they'd drink tea in the house, the parrot would enter the dining room and would climb with his beak and feet via the tablecloth to eat bread soaked in milk. the parrot liked tea with milk very much.

Pedrito would spend so much time with the kids, who would say so many things to him, that he learned to speak. He would say: "Good day, little parrot!" "Tasty bread with milk!" "Bread with milk for Pedrito!" He would say other things, too, that people shouldn't say to each other because parrots — like kids — learn bad words very easily.

When it would rain, Pedrito would say to himself a good portion of these words in a quiet voice. When the rain would finish, he would fly away, squawking like a crazy-bird.

He was, as can be seen, a very happy parrot which, in addition to being free, as all birds desire to be, also had, like rich people, his "five o'clock tea". Nevertheless, in the middle of this happiness, it happened that one afternoon, the sun finally came out after five rainy days, and Pedrito was flying squawking:

"What a nice day, little parrot! Tasty bread with milk! The leg, Pedrito!..."

He didn't fly far before he saw beneath him — very far below — the Parana River, which seemed like a distant and vast white cord. He continued flying and flying until he finally seated himself on a tree to rest.

Suddenly, he saw two green lights like enormous lightning bugs between the branches on the ground.

"What could that be?" the parrot said to himself. "Tasty bread with milk! What might that be? Good day, Pedrito!"

The parrot would always speak like this — like all parrots do — confusing words, and at times it was difficult to understand him. As he was very curious, he went descending from branch to branch until bringing himself closer. Then he saw that those two green lights were the eyes of a jaguar who was crouched down, staring at him, but Pedrito was so pleased with the nice day that he didn't have any fear.

"Good day, jaguar!" he said to him. "The leg, Pedrito!"

The jaguar, with that terribly rough voice that he has, responded to him:

"Good day!"

"Good day, jaguar!" repeated the parrot. "Tasty bread with milk! Tasty bread with milk! Tasty bread with milk!"

He would say, "tasty bread with milk!" so much because it was already the fourth hour of the afternoon and he was desperate to drink tea with milk. The parrot had forgotten that the animals of the jungle don't drink tea with milk and because of this he invited the jaguar to tea.

"Tasty tea with milk!" he said to him. "Good day, Pedrito! Do you want to drink tea with milk with me, friendly jaguar?" The jaguar got angry because he believed that the parrot was making fun of him and; furthermore, as he was hungry, he wanted to eat the talkative bird. He answered him:

"Well! Come a little closer because I'm deaf!"

The jaguar wasn't deaf. What he wanted was that Pedrito might come close enough to grab him with a swipe of his claws. The parrot wasn't thinking except on the satisfaction that they'd have at home when he might show up to drink tea with milk with that fascinating friend. He flew another branch closer to the ground.

"Tasty bread with milk at home!" he repeated, squawking as much as he could.

"Closer! I don't hear you!" responded the jaguar with his rough voice.

The parrot approached a little more and said:

"Tasty tea with milk!"

"Closer still!" repeated the jaguar.

The poor parrot approached even more and in that moment the jaguar made a terrible jump, as high as a house, and reached Pedrito with the tip of his claws. He didn't manage to kill him, but he violently removed all the feathers from his back and from his whole tail. Not a single feather remained on his tail.

"Take that!" roared the jaguar. "Go to drink tea with milk..."

The parrot, squawking from pain and fear, went flying from there, but he could not fly well because he didn't have his tail which is what birds use to guide themselves. He flew falling down in the air from one side to another, and all the birds that he'd meet on the way would distance themselves, scared of his strange behavior.

At last he was able to arrive at home, and the first thing that he did was look at himself in the mirror. Poor Pedrito! He was the strangest and most grotesque bird that could be: all plucked, without a tail, and trembling from cold. How was he going to show up in the dining room in that way? Then, he flew to the hollow that was in the trunk of a eucalyptus tree — which was like a cave — and he hid himself in the bottom, trembling from cold and disgrace.

Meanwhile, in the dining room, all were becoming anxious because of his absence:

"Where could Pedrito be?" they were saying.

They were calling:

"Pedrito! Tasty bread with milk, Pedrito! Tea with milk, Pedrito!" but Pedrito wouldn't move from his cave or respond at all. He stayed still and silent. They looked for him everywhere, but the parrot didn't show up. Then, everyone thought that Pedrito had died, and the kids began to cry.

Every afternoon at teatime, they would think on the parrot and would remember how much he liked to eat bread soaked in tea with milk. Poor Pedrito! Never again would they see him because he'd died! But Pedrito had not died. He was staying in his cave without letting himself be seen by anyone because he was feeling very humiliated from seeing himself unfeathered like a mouse. At night he would go down to eat and would go back up straightaway. Early in the morning, he would descend again, with great carefulness, and would go to look at himself in the mirror — always very sad because his feathers were greatly delaying in growing.

Finally one day — or one afternoon — the family being seated in the dining room at teatime, saw Pedrito enter very calmly, appearing as if nothing might have happened. Then everyone wanted to die — to die of pleasure when they saw him very alive and with gorgeous new feathers.

"Pedrito — little parrot!" they said to him. "What happened to you, Pedrito?! What bright feathers the little parrot has!" They didn't know that they were new feathers. Pedrito, very serious, said not one word. He wouldn't do anything except eat bread soaked in tea with milk, but he wouldn't say a single word.

Because of this, the owner of the house was very surprised when the parrot flew to his shoulder the following morning, chattering like a crazy-bird. In two minutes, Pedrito told him what had happened to him: the trip to the Paraguay River, his encounter with the jaguar, and the rest; and he would conclude each event singing:

"Not a feather on the tail of Pedrito! Not even a feather! Not even a feather!"

Then he invited the man to go hunt the jaguar between the two of them.

The owner of house, who was going in that very moment to buy a jaguar skin that he wanted for the stove of his dining room, was very pleased to be able to have one for free. Returning to enter into the house in order to grab the shotgun, he started the trip with Pedrito to the Paraguay River. They decided that when Pedrito would see the jaguar, he would distract him by chatting so that the man might be able to slowly approach with the shotgun.

So it happened. The parrot, seated on the branch of the same tree as before, chattered and chattered, watching all sides at the same time in order to see if he might see the jaguar. Finally he heard a sound of broken branches, and suddenly he saw beneath the tree two green lights fixed on him: they were the eyes of the jaguar.

Then the parrot began to shout:

"Pretty day! Tasty bread with milk! Tasty tea with milk! Do you want tea with milk?"

The jaguar, very angry to recognize that plucked parrot that he believed to be dead and that now had super nice feathers, swore that this time he wouldn't escape him and responded in his rough voice:

"Come closer! I'm deaf!"

The parrot flew another branch closer, always chattering:

"Tasty bread with milk!... He's at the foot of this tree!..."

Upon hearing these last words, the jaguar launched a roar and jumped up.

"With whom are you speaking?" he bellowed. "To whom have you said that I'm at the foot of this tree?"

"To nobody, to nobody!" squawked the parrot. "Good day, Pedrito! The leg, little parrot!"

And he continued chatting and jumping from branch to branch and approaching, but he had said, "he's at the foot of this tree" in order to warn the man, who was inching closer in a crouched position with the shotgun at the shoulder.

Then a moment arrived in which the parrot couldn't approach anymore without falling into the jaguar's mouth, and he squawked:

"Tasty bread with milk! Attention!"

"Closer still!" roared the jaguar, and he crouched in order to jump.

"Tasty tea with milk! Careful, he's going to jump!"

Then the jaguar—indeed—jumped. He made an enormous jump that the parrot avoided by launching himself into the air like a bullet at the same time. Also, in that same instant, the man, who had the barrel of the shotgun against a trunk in order to aim more true, shot the shotgun, and nine bullets entered into the body of the jaguar, who then launched a howl that made the entire mountain tremble and fell dead. What squawks of joy gave the parrot! He was crazy with happiness because he had avenged himself—and well avenged—of that super grotesque animal that had removed his feathers!

The man was also very glad because to kill a jaguar is a difficult thing; furthermore, he had the skin for the stove of the dining room.

When they arrived at home, all realized why Pedrito had been so much time hidden in the hollow of the tree, and everyone congratulated him for the heroism that he'd had.

Since then they lived very happily, but the parrot didn't forget what the jaguar had done to him: every afternoon, when he would enter into the dining room in order to drink tea, he would always approach the skin of the jaguar that was laid in front of the stove, and he would invite it to drink tea with milk.

"Tasty bread with milk!" he would say to it. "Do you want tea with milk? bread with milk for the jaguar!"

Then everyone would die of laughter. Pedrito also.

The End

The Lazy Bee

There was once a bee in a beehive that didn't want to work —
that is to say that it would go from tree to tree in order to
drink the nectar of the flowers, but instead of saving it and
converting it into honey, she would drink all of it.

It was a lazy bee. Every morning, as soon as the sun was
warming the air, the little bee would look through the door of
the beehive, would see that there was good weather, would
clean itself with its legs like a fly, and would shoot off then,
pleased with the nice day. She would happily fly from flower
to flower, would enter into the beehive, would leave once
again, and so would spend all day. Meanwhile the other bees
were killing themselves working in order to fill the beehive
with honey, since honey is the food of the baby bees.

As bees are very serious, they started to get disgusted because
of the conduct of the lazy sister. Now, in the door of the
beehives there are always some bees that are of guard in order
to make sure that other insects don't enter (such as beetles and
cockroaches) the beehive. These bees are normally very old
and with great life experience, and they have bald backs
because they've lost all their hairs.

One day, they stopped the lazy bee when she was going to
enter and they told her:

"Companion: it's necessary that you work because, as bees, we
should work."

The little bee answered:

"I go about all day flying and I tire myself out greatly."

"It's not a question of whether you tire yourself out greatly" they responded, "but of that you might work a little. This is the first warning that we make to you."

After saying this, they let her pass, but the lazy bee didn't behave herself. The following evening, the bees that were on guard told her:

"One has to work, sister."

She responded straightaway:

"One of these days I'm going to do it!"

"It's not a question of you doing it one of these days," they responded to her, "but of that you do it tomorrow. Remind yourself of this."

Then they let her pass.

At nightfall, the same thing happened again. Before they could say something to her, the little bee exclaimed:

"Yes, yes sisters! I already remember what I've promised!"

"It's not a question of you reminding yourself of the promised thing" they responded to her, but of you working. Today is the 19th of April: try tomorrow to bring at least one drop of honey. Now, pass."

After they said this, they parted in order to let her enter, but the 20th of April passed in vain like all the other days. The only difference was that at nightfall the weather became bad and the air became cold.

The lazy little bee flew quickly toward her beehive. She was thinking of the warmth that would be inside, but when she tried to enter, the bees that were on guard stopped her.

"Don't enter!" they said to her coldly.

"I want to enter!" exclaimed the little bee. "This is my beehive."

"This is the beehive of some poor hard-working bees," the others answered her. "There isn't entrance for lazy ones."

"Tomorrow I'm definitely going to work!" insisted the little bee.

"There's no tomorrow for those that don't work," responded the very wise bees.

After saying this, they pushed her outside.

The little bee, without knowing what to do, flew a while longer, but the night was already arriving and she couldn't see. She tried to rest upon a leaf, but she fell to the ground. Her body was paralyzed because of the cold air and she couldn't fly anymore.

Then, she dragged herself over the ground and went over top and underneath the little sticks and rocks, which seemed like mountains to her, and she arrived at the door of the beehive when cold raindrops were starting to fall.

"Oh God!" she exclaimed desperately. "It's going to rain and I'm going to die of cold."

And she tried entering into the beehive, but again they closed the way to her.

"Pardon me!" grumbled the bee to herself. "Let me enter!"

"It's already too late," they responded to her.

"Please, sisters! I'm tired!"

"It's even later."

"Companions, for compassion! I'm cold!"

"Impossible."

"For the last time! I'm going to die!"

Then, they told her:

"No, you won't die. You'll learn in a single night what is the rest earned from work. Go from here."

Then they threw her out.

Then, trembling from cold and staggering with her wet wings, the bee dragged herself forward. She dragged herself until suddenly she fell through a hole to the bottom of a cave.

She thought that she was never going to finish falling. Finally, she arrived at the bottom and found herself suddenly before a viper—a green snake with a yellow-colored back that was watching her while curled up and prepared to launch itself upon her.

In reality, that cave was the hollow of a fallen tree that the snake had selected for its den.

Snakes eat bees since they like them a lot. Because of this, the little bee, upon finding herself before her enemy, murmured with her eyes closed:

"Goodbye, my life! This is the last hour that I will see the light." Then with great surprise, the snake not only didn't eat her, but said to her:

"How are you, little bee? You must not be very hard-working to be here at these hours."

"It's the truth," murmured the bee. "I don't work and it's my mistake."

"Being so," mocked the snake, "I'm going to remove from the earth a bad insect like you. I'm going to eat you, bee."

Then the bee, trembling, exclaimed:

"That's not just, it's not just! It's not right for you to eat me because you're stronger than I am. Man knows what is justice."

"Ah, ah!" exclaimed the snake, curling herself up rapidly. "Do you know men well? Do you think that the men that take away the honey from you are more just, you great big fool?"

"No, it's not because of that that they take away the honey from us," responded the bee.

"And why, then?"

"Because they're more intelligent."

So said the little bee, but the snake fell to the floor laughing and exclaimed:

"Well! With justice or without it, I'm going to eat you... prepare yourself."

Then she threw herself back in order to launch herself upon the bee, but the bee exclaimed:

"You do that because your intelligence is less than my intelligence."

"I less intelligent than you, fly?" laughed the snake.

"So it is," affirmed the bee.

"Well then," said the snake, "let's see. Let's make two tryouts. The one that makes the stranger tryout wins. If I win, I eat you."

"And if I win?" asked the little bee.

"If you win," answered her enemy, "you have the right to spend the night here until it's daytime. OK?"

"Accepted," answered the bee.

The snake laughed again because a thing had occurred to her that a bee never would be able to do, and like so it did it:

She went for an instant outside, so rapidly that the bee didn't have time to move, and she returned carrying a capsule of seeds from a eucalyptus tree that was at the side of the den.

Men make those capsules dance in the air like tops and they call them little eucalyptus tops.

"That is what I'm going to do," said the snake. "Watch!"

She coiled her tail around the little top like a wire and she uncoiled it at full velocity with so much speed that the little top kept dancing and spinning around like crazy.

"That tryout is very nice and I will never be able to do it."

"Then I eat you," exclaimed the snake.

"One moment! I can't do that, but I do a thing that nobody does."

"What is that?"

"Disappear."

"How?" exclaimed the snake while making a surprise jump. "Disappear without going out of here?"

"Without going out of here."

"And without hiding yourself in the ground?"

"Without hiding myself in the ground."

"Well then, do it! And if you don't do it, I'll eat you straightaway," said the snake.

While the little top was dancing, the bee had had time to examine the cave and had seen a little plant with big leaves that was growing there.

The bee moved herself closer to the little plant, taking care not touch it, and said like so:

"Now it's my turn, Mrs. Snake. Do me the favor of turning around and counting to three. When you say "three," look for me everywhere, No longer will I be anymore!"

So it happened indeed. The snake quickly said: "one... two... three," and it turned around and opened its mouth as wide as it could... surprise: there was not anybody there. She looked up, down, at all sides, she perused over the little plant and examined everything with her tongue. It was in vain: the bee had disappeared.

Then, the snake understood that if her tryout with the little top was very good, the tryout of the bee was simply incredible. What had she done to herself? Where was she? She didn't have a way of finding her.

"Well!" she exclaimed at last. "I lose. Where are you?"

A voice that was barely heard — the voice of the little bee — came out of the middle of the cave.

"You're not going to do anything to me?" said the voice. "Can I count on your word?"

"Yes," responded the snake. "I swear it to you. Where are you?"

"Here," responded the little bee, appearing suddenly from a closed leaf of the little plant.

What had happened? A very simple thing: the little plant in question was what is known as a sensitive plant, which is also very common here in Buenos Aires. It has the peculiarity that its leaves close upon the least contact. Except that this adventure was happening in Misiones, where the vegetation is very rich; in consequence, the leaves of the sensitive plants are very large and, upon contact with the bee, the leaves closed and hid the insect completely.

The snake was not very intelligent, since it never noticed this phenomenon; but the bee had noticed it and utilized it as an advantage in order to save her life.

The snake didn't say anything, but was very irritated upon losing, so much so that the bee spent all night reminding her enemy of the oath that she had made to respect her life. It was a long night — endless — that the two spent up against the tallest side of the cave because it had started to rain very hard and the water was entering inside like a river.

It was very cold. Furthermore, the darkness was predominating inside. Every once in awhile, the snake would feel urges to launch itself upon the bee. In those moments, the bee was thinking that the end of her life would arrive.

The little bee never believed that one night could be so cold, so long, so horrible. She was remembering her past life, when she would sleep night after night in the beehive, nice and warm, and she was crying in silence.

When day arrived and the sun came out because the weather had improved, the little bee flew and cried once again in silence before the door of the beehive that was made by the effort of the family. The bees on guard let her pass without saying anything to her because they understood that the one who was returning was not the lazy bee, but a bee that had learned in just one night a difficult life lesson.

So it went, indeed. After that, nobody gathered so much pollen like her nor produced so much honey. When summer ended, and the end of her days also arrived, she still had time to give a last lesson before dying to all the young bees of the hive:

"It's not our intelligence, but it's our work, which makes us so strong. Only once did I utilize my intelligence, and it was in order to save my life. I wouldn't have needed to do this if I had worked like everyone else. I've tired myself out so much flying from here to there as if I was working. What I needed was the notion of duty that I acquired that night.

"Work, companions, thinking on the end to which the others direct our efforts. The happiness of everyone is very superior to the tiredness of each one. This men call ideal and they have reason to. There isn't another philosophy in the life of a man and of a bee."

The End

The Passage of the Yabebiri

In the Yabebiri river that is in Misiones, there are many
stingrays. "Yabebiri" means "river of the stingrays". There are
so many, that it's sometimes dangerous to stick a foot in the
water. I met a man whom a stingray stung in the foot and who
had to go about with difficulty, dragging his feet for three
kilometers, in order to arrive at his house: the man was crying
and falling down from pain. It's one of the strongest pains that
one can feel.

Since there are also many other fish in the Yabebiri, some men
go to fish for them with bombs of dynamite. They throw a
bomb to the river and they kill millions of fish. All the fish that
are near die, although they are as big as a house. The very
small ones that don't serve for anything also all die.

Once, a man went to live there, and he didn't want for them to
throw bombs of dynamite because he had compassion for the
very small fish. He wasn't opposed to them fishing in the river
in order to eat, but he didn't want for them to needlessly kill
millions of small fish. The men that would throw bombs got
angry at first; however, as the man had a serious character —
although he was very good — the others went from there to
fish in another place and all the fish were very glad. They
were so glad and thankful that they would salute the man as
soon as he would approach the bank. When he would go by
the coast smoking, the stingrays would follow him while
dragging themselves through the mud, very glad to
accompany their friend. He didn't know anything about that
and was living happily in that place.

One afternoon, a fox arrived by running up to the Yabebiri
and stuck his paws into the water and shouted:

"Oh, stingrays! Quickly! Here comes your friend. He's wounded."

The stingrays that heard him swam anxiously to the bank. They asked the fox:

"What is happening? Where is the man?"

"Here he comes!" shouted the fox again. "He's fought against a jaguar! The jaguar is coming pursuing him! Surely he's going to cross to the isle! Give him passage because he's a good man!"

"Already we believe you! Already we believe you and we're going to give him passage!" answered the stingrays. "The jaguar isn't going to pass!"

"Careful with him!" still the fox shouted. "Don't forget that he's the jaguar!"

Then with a jump, the fox entered again into the jungle.

Scarcely was he finished doing this when the man pushed aside the branches and appeared all bloody with his shirt torn. The blood was running down his head and his body as far as his pants and from his pants the blood was falling to the sand.

He advanced, staggering toward the bank, since he was very hurt, and he entered the river. As soon as he put one foot in the water, the stingrays that were grouped-up there parted from his way, and the man crossed unto the isle with the water almost up to his neck, without a stingray having stung him. When he arrived, he fell unconscious on the same sand because of the great quantity of blood that he'd lost.

The stingrays had not even had time to console their dying friend when a terrible roar made them tremble in the water.

"The jaguar! The jaguar!" shouted everyone, launching themselves like torpedoes to the bank.

Indeed, the jaguar that had fought with the man and that was coming pursuing him had arrived to the shore of the Yabebiri. The animal was also very hurt and blood was running down his head and all over his body. He saw the man fallen as if he were dead on the isle and, launching a roar of anger, he threw himself into the water in order to finish killing him. Nevertheless, as soon as he had stuck a paw into the water, he felt as if six or seven terrible claws might've cut his paws and he leapt back: they were the stingrays that were defending the passage of the river and they'd stung him with all their force with their tail stingers.

The jaguar kept roaring from pain with his paw in the air and, upon seeing that all the water from the bank was foamy as if they had agitated the mud of the bottom, he comprehended that it was the stingrays that didn't want to let him pass. Then, he shouted super angrily:

"Ah, I already know what you are! It's you, detestable stingrays! Get out of the way!"

"We won't leave!" responded the stingrays.

"Get out!" roared the jaguar.

"We won't leave! He is a good man! You don't have a right to kill him!"

"He has wounded me!" complained the jaguar.

"The two of you have wounded each other! Those are problems of you all in the jungle! Here he's under our protection!... You will not pass!"

"Yes, I will pass!" roared the jaguar for the last time.

"Neither now, nor ever!" responded the stingrays.

(They said "neither now, nor ever" because so speak those that speak Guarani as in Misiones).

"We'll see!" bellowed still the jaguar. Then, he backed up and prepared to make an enormous leap.

The jaguar knew that the stingrays are almost always on the bank and he was thinking that if he would manage to make a very large jump, possibly he wouldn't find more stingrays in the middle of the river and he could thereby eat the man who was dying.

The stingrays had foreseen it and all ran to the middle of the river, spreading the word:

"Out from the bank!" they were shouting under the water. "Inward! To the canal! To the canal!"

In a second, the army of stingrays launched itself inside of the river to defend the passage at the same time that the jaguar was making his enormous leap and was falling in the middle of the water. He fell crazy with joy because he didn't feel any stings right away and believed that the stingrays had all remained in the bank, mislead. But as soon as he swam one step, a true rainfall of stings, like lances of pain, stopped him straightaway: it was once again the army of stingrays that was wounding him on the paws with stings.

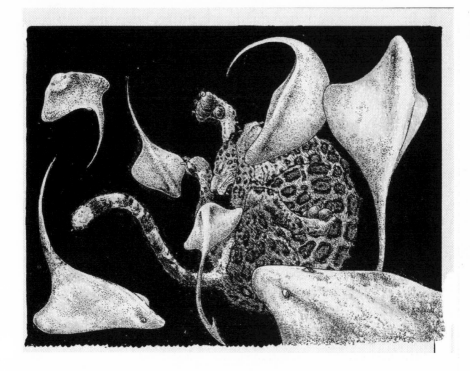

The jaguar wanted to continue; nevertheless, the pain was so terrible that he gave a shout and backed away swimming like crazy to the bank. He threw himself on the sand sidelong since he couldn't swim or move anymore because of his suffering. He was breathing deeply as if he were super tired.

What was happening is that the jaguar was poisoned by the stingrays.

Although they had triumphed against the jaguar, the stingrays were not comforted because they were afraid that the female jaguar might come — his companion — and other jaguars... They could not defend the passage anymore.

Indeed, the jungle howled again and the female appeared, who went crazy with anger upon seeing the jaguar thrown sidelong on the sand. She also saw the water that was foaming because of the movement of the stingrays and she approached the river. Almost touching the water with her mouth, she shouted:

"Stingrays! I want passage!"

"There's no passage!" responded the stingrays.

"Not one single stingray is going to remain with a tail if you don't give passage!" roared the female.

"Even if we remain without tails, you won't pass!" they responded.

"For the last time, I will pass!"

"Neither now, nor ever!" shouted the stingrays.

The female — super angry — had a paw stuck in the water without meaning to and a stingray, approaching slowly, stung her with its stinger on her paw. At the howl of the animal's pain, the stingrays responded while laughing:

"It seems that we still have tails!"

The female had had an idea and with that idea in her head she moved herself away from there. She skirted the river upstream without saying a word.

The stingrays understood the plan of their enemy this time also. The plan of their enemy was this: to pass the river by the other part where the stingrays wouldn't know that they should defend the passage. Suddenly, the stingrays felt extremely anxious.

"She's going to pass the river upstream!" they shouted. "We don't want her to kill the man! We have to defend our friend!"

So they stirred desperately amidst the mud until clouding up the river.

"What do we do?!" they said. "We don't know how to swim quickly... The female is going to pass before the stingrays there know that they should defend the passage at all costs!"

They didn't know what to do, until a very intelligent little stingray suddenly said:

"I know what we have to do! Let's ask the golden fish to go! The golden fish are our friends! They swim more quickly than anybody!"

"That is it!" shouted everyone. "Let's ask the golden fish to go!"

In an instant, the word spread and, in another instant, they saw eight or ten columns of golden fish. A true army of golden fish was swimming at full velocity upstream: they went making foam in the water like torpedos.

In spite of everything, as soon as they had time to ask that the passage might be closed to the jaguars, the female had already swum and was already arriving to the isle.

The army of stingrays had already swum to the other bank and just before the female made it to the other side, the stingrays launched themselves against her paws, wounding them with stings. The animal, super angry and crazy from pain, was howling and jumping in the water and making clouds of water fly; however, the stingrays continued launching themselves against her paws, closing to her the passage in such a way that the female had to turn around, swim again and throw herself to the bank with her four paws terribly swollen. Over there she could not go to eat the man.

The stingrays were also very tired. What is worse, the jaguar and the female had ended up getting up and entering the jungle.

What are they going to do? This made the stingrays very restless, and they had a long meeting. Finally, they said:

"We already know what they'll do: they'll seek out the other jaguars, and all of them are going to come... all the jaguars will come and pass!"

"Neither now, nor ever!" shouted the youngest stingrays, who didn't have as much experience.

"Yes, they'll pass, little companions!" responded the older ones sadly. "If they are many they'll end up passing... Let's consult our friend."

All went to see the man, since they had not had time yet to do it because they had been defending the passage of the river.

The man was still lying down since he had lost a lot of blood, but he could speak and move a little bit. In an instant, the stingrays told him what had happened and how they had defended the passage from the jaguars that wanted to eat him. The wounded man was moved greatly by the loyalty of the stingrays that had saved his life and he extended his hand with true affection to the stingrays that were closest to him. He said then:

"There's no remedy! If the jaguars are many and they want to pass, they'll pass..."

"They won't pass!" said the little stingrays. "You are our friend and they're not going to pass!"

"Yes, they'll pass, little companions!" said the man speaking in a quiet voice:

"The only way would be if someone went to my house for my Winchester rifle and a lot of bullets... I don't have any friends in the river, outside of the fish... And none of you know how to walk over the ground."

"What do we do then?" said the stingrays anxiously.

"Let's see, let's see..." Then said the man, passing his hand along his whiskers, as if he were remembering something. "I had a friend... a capybara who was educated in my house and who would play with my children... One day he returned once again to the jungle and I believe that he was living here, in the Yabebiri... I don't know where he'll be..."

The stingrays then gave a shout of joy:

"We already know! We know him! He has his den on the tip of the isle! He spoke to us once of you! We're going to search for him straightaway!"

Said and done: a very large golden fish swam downriver to look for the capybara. Meanwhile, the man dissolved a drop of dry blood in the center of his hand and took a stick and a dry leaf in order to write a letter with them. He wrote this letter: it's very important that you give my Winchester rifle and twenty-five bullets to the capybara.

As soon as the man finished writing, the entire mountain trembled with a dull roar: it was all the jaguars that were approaching to initiate the fight... an army of jaguars. The stingrays carried the letter with their heads outside of the water so that it wouldn't get wet, and they gave it to the capybara, which left running through the field to carry it to the man's house.

It was about time because, although the roars were still far off, they were approaching quickly. The stingrays gathered, then, the golden fish that were awaiting orders and shouted to them:

"Quickly, companions! Roam the whole river and spread the word of alarm! Let all the stingrays be quick throughout the river! Let everyone meet around the isle! We'll see if they're going to pass!"

The army of golden fish swam straightaway upriver and downriver, making foam in the water because of the speed that they bore.

Not a stingray remained throughout the Yabebiri that didn't receive the order to concentrate itself on the banks of the river around the isle. From everywhere, from between rocks, from amidst the mud, from the mouths of the tributaries, from the entire Yabebiri the stingrays were coming to defend the passage against the jaguars. In front of the isle, the golden fish were crossing back and forth at full speed.

It was about time, since once again an immense roar made the water of the bank tremble, and the jaguars were congregating on the coast.

They were many... it seemed that all the jaguars from Misiones were there. The entire Yabebiri was also abounding in stingrays, which launched themselves to the bank, disposed to defend the passage unto death.

"Give passage to the jaguars!" roared all the jaguars.

"There's no passage!" responded the stingrays.

"Give passage, again!"

"You won't pass!" confirmed the stingrays.

"There's not going to remain a stingray nor son of a stingray nor grandson of a stingray if you don't give passage!"

"It's possible!" responded the stingrays. "But neither the jaguars nor the sons of the jaguars nor the grandsons of the jaguars nor all the jaguars of the earth will pass through here!"

So responded the stingrays. Then, the jaguars roared for the last time:

"We ask for passage!"

"Neither now, nor ever!"

Then the battle started. With enormous jumps, the jaguars launched themselves to the water. They all fell upon a true floor of stingrays. The stingrays attacked their paws with stings and with each wound the jaguars would launch a roar of pain, but they were defending themselves with swipes, swiping at the water like crazy. The stingrays were flying through the air, cut by the claws of the jaguars.

The Yabebiri looked like a river of blood. Hundreds of the stingrays were dying; nevertheless, the jaguars were receiving terrible wounds also and would move themselves away to attend to themselves and to howl on the beach, horribly swollen. The stingrays, ruined by the paws of the jaguars, wouldn't stop: they were coming without ceasing to defend the passage. Some would fly through the air, would return to fall to the river and would launch themselves again against the army of jaguars.

This terrible fight persisted for half an hour. At the end of that half hour, all the jaguars were once again on the beach, seated from tiredness and roaring from pain. Not even a single one had passed.

The stingrays were also undone from tiredness. Many — a great many — had died. Those that remained alive said:

"We can't resist two attacks like this. Let the golden fish go to seek reinforcements! Let all the stingrays of the Yabebiri come straightaway!"

So the golden fish swam once again upriver and downriver and went so quickly that they were making foam in the water like torpedoes.

Then, the stingrays went to see the man.

"We won't be able to resist anymore!" the stingrays said to him sadly. Some stingrays were even crying because they saw that they could not save their friend.

"Go from here, stingrays!" responded the wounded man. "Leave me alone! You have done much already for me! Let the jaguars pass!"

"Neither now, nor ever!" shouted the stingrays in a single shout. "While there's a single stingray alive in the Yabebiri — our river — we'll defend the good man who defended us before!"

The wounded man exclaimed gladly:

"Stingrays! I am at the point of dying, and I can barely speak; but I assure you that as soon as the Winchester rifle arrives, we'll have a killing for a long while... this I assure you!"

"Yes, we already know it!" answered the stingrays excitedly.

They couldn't finish speaking, since the battle was recommencing. Indeed: the jaguars, that already had rested, got up, crouching like those who are going to jump, and roared:

"For the last time, and once and for all: give us passage!"

"Neither now, nor ever!" responded the stingrays launching themselves to the bank. But the jaguars had jumped at the same time to the water and recommenced the terrible fight. The entire Yabebiri, now from bank to bank, was red from blood, and the blood was making foam on the sand of the beach. The stingrays were flying, destroyed, through the air, and the jaguars were howling from pain; however, nobody would back up one step.

The jaguars not only wouldn't back up, but were advancing. In vain, the army of golden fish was swimming at full speed upriver and downriver calling to the stingrays. The stingrays had expired: all were fighting by the isle and one out of every two had died already. Those that remained were all wounded, without strength.

They comprehended then that they wouldn't be able to resist a minute more, and that the jaguars would pass. The poor stingrays launched themselves for the last time against the jaguars; however, all was already useless: five jaguars were already swimming toward the shore of the isle. The stingrays, desperate, shouted:

"To the isle! Let's all go to the other bank!"

It was too late: two more jaguars had jumped in to swim, and, in an instant, all the jaguars were in the middle of the river, and not more than their heads could be seen.

Also in that moment, a little animal — a poor little animal with a lot of red hair — was crossing the Yabebiri, swimming at full force: it was the capybara, which was arriving to the isle, carrying the Winchester rifle and the bullets upon his head so that they wouldn't get wet.

The man gave a great shout of joy because he would have time to enter into defense of the stingrays. He asked the capybara to push him with his head in order to station himself sidelong, since he alone could not do it and, in this position now, he armed the Winchester rifle with great speed.

The stingrays, being clawed up, undone, broken and bloody, saw with desperation that they had lost the battle and that the jaguars were going to eat their poor wounded friend. They saw that the jaguar that was going in front already was stepping on the sand, and it made a great leap, but in that precise moment, they heard a loud noise, and the jaguar fell dead with his head punctured from a shot.

"Bravo, bravo!" exclaimed the stingrays, crazy from happiness. "The man has the Winchester rifle! We're saved!"

They were clouding up the water, truly crazy from joy. The man continued shooting calmly, and each shot was a new jaguar dead. Each time that a jaguar would fall dead, launching a roar, the stingrays would respond with great shakes of their tails.

One after another the jaguars were dying by the Winchester rifle. That lasted only two minutes. One after another they went from there to the bottom of the river, and there the piranhas ate them. Some floated afterward; then the golden fish accompanied them up to the Parana river, eating them and making the water splash in their happiness.

In no time, the stingrays, which have many children, became as numerous as before. The man got better and was so grateful to the stingrays that had saved his life that he went to live at the isle. There, in the summer nights, he liked to stretch out on the beach and smoke by the light of the moon. The stingrays would slowly talk, showing him to the fish that didn't know him, and they would tell them about the great battle that, allied to this man, they had had once against the jaguars.

The End

The Giant Tortoise

There was once a man that lived in Buenos Aires and was very happy because he was a strong and hard-working man, but one day he got sick and the doctors told him that only by going from there to the jungle could he get better. He didn't want to go because he had little brothers to whom he would give to eat, but each day he was getting sicker. Then his friend, who was the director of the zoo, said to him one day:

"You are my friend and you're a good and hard-working man. I want you to go from here to live in the jungle and do a lot of exercise outdoors in order to get better. Since you have good aim with the shotgun, you'll be able to hunt animals in the jungle in order to bring me the skins, and I will give you money in advance so that your little brothers will be able to eat well."

The sick man accepted and went from there to live far away in the jungle, farther even than Misiones. It was very hot there and this made him well. He lived alone in the jungle. He would eat birds and animals of the jungle that he'd hunt with his shotgun; for dessert, he'd eat fruits, like bananas and oranges. He would sleep under the trees, and when there was bad weather he would construct a five-minute hut with palm leaves and would spend the time there, seated and smoking, very pleased in the middle of the jungle that was howling with the wind and the rain.

He had joined together the animal skins and would carry them on his shoulders. Also he had grabbed many poisonous vipers and would carry them alive inside of a big gourd because there there are gourds as big as small barrels of gasoline there. The man got his color back, he was strong, and he had his appetite. One day, when he was very hungry because he had not hunted anything in two days, he saw an enormous jaguar on the bank of a great lagoon that wanted to eat a tortoise and was placing it on its side in order to stick a paw inside and remove its meat with its claws. Upon seeing the man, the jaguar launched a scary roar and lept toward him; nevertheless, the hunter, who had good aim, aimed between its eyes and shot it in the head. Afterward, he removed his skin. It was so large that it could only serve to fully occupy the floor of a room.

"Now," the man said to himself. "I'm going to eat tortoise, which is a very tasty meat."

When he approached the tortoise, he saw that it was already wounded. It had its head almost separated from its neck, and its head was hanging by a little bit of flesh.

In spite of the hunger that he was feeling, the man had compassion for the poor tortoise and dragged it with a vine up to his hut and he put bands on its head that he took from his shirt, because he didn't have anything else besides a single shirt, and he didn't have medical materials. He had dragged it because the tortoise was immense — as tall as a chair — and it was as heavy as a man.

The tortoise stayed in the hut and spent days and days there without moving.

The man would treat it every day and afterward would give it pats of affection with his hand upon its back.

The tortoise got better at last, but afterward it was the man who got sick. He had a fever and his entire body was hurting him.

Afterward, he could not get up anymore. The fever was rising continually and he was very thirsty. The man understood that he was seriously ill and spoke in a loud voice although he was alone, because he had a high fever.

"I'm going to die," the man said. "I'm alone. No longer can I get up anymore and I don't have anyone to give me water. I'm going to die here from hunger and thirst."

After a while, the fever rose even more, and he lost consciousness, but the tortoise had heard him and understood what the hunter was saying. She thought:

"The man didn't eat me before, although he was very hungry, and he treated me. I am going to treat him now."

Then, she went to the lagoon, sought a small gourd, filled it with water, and gave to the man to drink of it, who was outstretched upon the floor and dying of thirst. Straightaway, she began to look for tasty roots and tender herbs that she brought to the man so that he might eat. The man would eat without knowing who was giving him the food because he was delirious with the fever and he wasn't recognizing anyone.

Every morning, the tortoise would roam the jungle, looking for more and more tasty roots in order to give them to the man, but she felt unable to climb the trees in order to bring him fruits, like bananas and oranges.

The hunter ate in this way for days and days without knowing who was giving him the food, and then one day he recovered his consciousness. He looked to all sides and saw that he was alone, since there was not anyone else other than himself and the tortoise, who was an animal. He said, once again, in a loud voice:

"I'm alone in the jungle, the fever is going to return again and I'm going to die here because only in Buenos Aires are there remedies for curing me, but I'll never be able to go like this and I'm going to die here."

As he had said it, the fever returned that afternoon stronger than before and, again, he lost consciousness, but also this time the tortoise had heard him and said to herself:

"If he stays here in the jungle, he's going to die because there are not any remedies: I have to carry him to Buenos Aires."

This said, she cut thin and strong vines which are like cords, she laid down the man with much care on top of her back, and held him well with the vines so that he wouldn't fall down. She secured well the shotgun, the skins, and the gourd with vipers, and finally she obtained what she wanted. Without waking the hunter, she then began the journey.

The tortoise, carrying him in this way, walked, walked, and walked during day and night. She passed by jungles, fields, swam rivers as wide as six kilometers from one side to the other, and crossed lagoons where she would almost sink— always with the dying man on top. After nine or ten hours of walking, she would stop, untie the cords, and would lay down the man with much care in a place where there was very dry grass.

She would then go to look for water and tender roots and would give them to the sick man. She would eat too, although she was so tired that what she wanted above all was to sleep.

At times, she had to walk in the sun and, as it was summer, the hunter's fever was rising so much that he was hallucinating and dying of thirst. He would shout: "Water! Water!" every minute. Each time, the tortoise had to give him to drink.

Like so she went about for days and days, week after week. Each day they were closer to Buenos Aires, but also every day the tortoise was getting weaker. Every day she had less strength, although she would never cry. At times, she would stay stretched out, completely without strength, and the man would recover his consciousness partially. Then he would say in a loud voice:

"I'm going to die, I'm more and more sick and only in Buenos Aires could I get better, but I'm going to die here, alone in the jungle."

He believed that he was always in the hut because he wasn't conscious of anything. Then, the tortoise would get up, and would take up the path again. Then one day arrived — an afternoon — in which the poor tortoise could not walk anymore. She had arrived at the limit of her strength and could not continue anymore. She hadn't eaten for a week so that they could arrive sooner. She had no more strength for anything.

When night fell, she saw a light in the distance—a brightness that was illuminating the sky and she didn't know what it was. She felt more and more tired and closed her eyes in order to die together with the hunter. She was thinking with sadness that she had not been able to save the man that had been good to her; nevertheless, she was already in Buenos Aires and she didn't know it. That light that she saw in the sky was the shine of the city, and she was going to die when she was already at the end of her heroic journey. But a mouse of the city found the two travelers who were dying.

"What a tortoise!" said the mouse. "Never have I seen a tortoise so big. And that which you carry on your back, what is it? Is it sticks?"

"No," the tortoise responded to him with sadness. "It's a man."

"And where are you going with that man?" said the curious mouse.

"I'm going... I'm going... I was wanting to go to Buenos Aires," responded the poor tortoise with a voice so quiet that it could barely be heard; "nevertheless, we're going to die here because I will never arrive..."

"Ah, silly, silly!" said the little mouse, laughing. "Never have I seen a sillier tortoise! You've already made it to Buenos Aires! That light that you see there is Buenos Aires."

Upon hearing this, the tortoise felt it had an immense strength because she still had time to save the hunter, and so she restarted the march.

When it was still early morning, the zoo director saw a dirty and extremely skinny tortoise arrive, that was bringing, laid down on her back and held with vines so that he wouldn't fall down, a man that was dying. The man recognized his friend and went running to look for remedies with which the hunter was healed straightaway.

When the hunter realized how the tortoise had saved him, how she had made a journey of 1,600 kilometers so that he could be healed, he didn't want to separate himself from her. As he could not have her in his house because it was very small, the Zoo director promised to have her in the garden of the Zoo and care for her as if she were his daughter.

So it happened. The tortoise, happy and pleased with the affection that they have for her, goes about throughout the entire zoo garden. In fact, it's the same big tortoise that we see every day eating the grass around the cages of the mongooses.

The hunter goes to see her every afternoon, and she recognizes her friend from far away by his gait. They spend two hours together, and she never wants him to go from there without giving her a pat of affection on her back.

The End

The Flamingos' Stockings

One day, the vipers gave a great ball. They invited the frogs, the toads, the flamingos, the alligators, and the fish. The fish, as they don't walk, could not dance, but being that the dance was at the bank of the river, would stay on the sand and would applaud with their tails.

In order to adorn themselves well, the alligators had put necklaces of bananas on their necks and were smoking Paraguayan cigars. The toads had put scales of fish all over their bodies and would walk, shaking themselves as if they were swimming. Each time that they would pass very seriously by the bank of the river, the fish would shout at them and tease them.

The frogs had perfumed themselves all over their bodies and were walking on two feet. Furthermore, everyone was wearing a lightning bug hung from the neck, like a little lantern necklace. Those who were nicest of all were the vipers. All of them, without exception, were wearing dancer outfits, in the same color as each viper. The red vipers were wearing a red skirt; the green ones, a green skirt; the yellow ones, a different yellow skirt; and the rattlesnakes, a gray skirt with black and brown stripes because so is the color of rattlesnakes.

The most fascinating of all, though, were the coral vipers, who were wearing very long red, white, and black skirts. When the vipers would dance and make turns on the tips of their tails, all the guests would applaud like crazy.

Only the flamingos, who then had white legs and now have—just as before—a very long and irregular nose, were sad because, as they have very little intelligence, they had not known how to adorn themselves. They envied the outfits of everyone else and—above all—those of the coral vipers. Each time that a viper would pass in front of them, shaking their skirts, the flamingos would die of envy.

A flamingo said, then:

"I know what we're going to do. Let's put on red, white, and black stockings, and the coral vipers will fall in love with us."

And flying all together, they crossed the river and went to a store in the town.

"Knock, knock!" they knocked with their legs.

"Who is it?" Responded the shopkeeper.

"It's the flamingos. Do you have red, white, and black stockings?"

"No, there are none," answered the shopkeeper. "Are you crazy? Nowhere will you find stockings like that."

The flamingos then went to another store.

"Knock, knock! Do you have red, white, and black stockings?"

The shopkeeper answered:

"How do you say? red, white, and black? There aren't stockings like that anywhere. You are crazy. Who are you?"

"We're the flamingos," they responded.

Then the man said:

"Then, you are — with certainty — crazy flamingos."

They went to another store.

"Knock, knock! Do you have red, white, and black stockings?"

While cleaning with a broom, the shopkeeper shouted:

"Of what color? red, white, and black? Only to birds with great noses like you does it occur to ask for stockings like that. Leave right now!"

Then the man threw them out with the broom.

The flamingos checked all the stores in this way and everywhere they would be thrown out as crazy. Then an armadillo, who had gone to drink water at the river and wanted to make fun of the flamingos, made a big salute to them and said:

"Good night, flamingos! I know what you are looking for. You'll not find stockings like that in any store. Possibly there might be some in Buenos Aires, but you'd have to order them. The owl has stockings like this. Ask her for them and she will give you the red, white, and black stockings."

The flamingos gave him thanks and went flying from there to the cave of the owl. They said to her:

"Good night, owl! We came to ask you for some red, white, and black stockings. Today is the great ball of the vipers and if we put on those stockings, the coral vipers will fall in love with us."

"With much pleasure!" the owl responded. "Wait a second and I'll return straightaway."

She flew off, leaving the flamingos alone. After a time, she returned with the stockings, but they were not stockings, but coral viper skins — gorgeous skins taken from the vipers that the owl had hunted.

"Here are the stockings," the owl said to them. "Don't worry about anything except one single thing: dance all night, dance without stopping a moment, dance sidelong, from your beaks, headlong — however you wish — but don't stop for a moment because if you do, in place of dancing, you're going to cry."

The flamingos, since they are so foolish, didn't comprehend well what great danger there was for them in this and — crazy from joy — they put on the coral viper skins like stockings, inserting their legs inside of the skins, which were like tubes. Very glad, they went flying from there to the ball.

When they saw the flamingos with their gorgeous stockings, everyone was envious of them. The vipers wanted to dance solely with them, and, as the flamingos didn't stop moving their legs even for an instant, the vipers could not see well what those nice stockings were made of; nevertheless, little by little the vipers began to suspect something. When the flamingos would pass to the side of them dancing, they would crouch low to the ground in order to see better.

The coral vipers — especially — were very restless. They wouldn't take their eyes off of the stockings and would crouch low, also trying touch the legs of the flamingos with their tongues because the tongue of the vipers is like the hand of the people, but the flamingos were dancing and dancing without stopping, although they were super tired and could no longer dance anymore.

The coral vipers realized this. Straightaway, they asked for the little lanterns of the frogs, which were lightning bugs, and all waited together for when the flamingos might fall down from tiredness.

Effectively, a minute afterward, a flamingo that could no longer dance anymore danced upon the cigar of an alligator, staggered and fell sidelong. Straightaway, the coral vipers slithered with their little lanterns and illuminated the legs of the flamingo. They saw what the stockings were and gave a shout that was heard as far as the other bank of the Parana river.

"They aren't stockings!" shouted the vipers. "We know what they are! They've mislead us! The flamingos have killed our sisters and have put on their skins like stockings! The stockings that they have are from coral vipers!"

Upon hearing this, the flamingos, full of fear because they were discovered, tried to fly away; but they were so tired that they could not lift a single leg. Then the coral vipers launched themselves upon them and, curling themselves around their legs, destroyed the stockings with bites. They were very angry, and were biting their legs also so that they might die.

Furthermore, the coral vipers were sure that the flamingos were going to die because one out of every two — at the least — of the coral vipers that had bitten them was poisonous, but the flamingos didn't die. They ran to throw themselves to the water, feeling a massive pain. They shouted from pain, and their legs — which were white — were now red because of the venom of the vipers. They spent days and days like this and were always feeling terrible pain in their legs which were now in the color of blood because they were poisoned.

A very great amount of time has passed now, and the flamingos still spend almost all day with their red legs inserted in the water, trying to calm the pain that they feel in them.

At times they part themselves from the bank and take some steps by land in order to see how they find themselves, but the pains of the venom return straightaway, and they run to get in the water. At times, the pain that they feel is so great that they contract their legs and remain like this for entire hours because they can't extend them.

This is the story of the flamingos that before had white legs and now have red ones. All the fish know why this is and they make fun of them, but the flamingos, while they are healing themselves in the water, don't lose occasion of avenging themselves, eating each small fish that approaches to make fun of them.

The End

Made in the USA
Las Vegas, NV
31 December 2022

64415326R00055